Laws of

M000046231

The 7 Golden RULES of MILTON HERSHEY

Executive Books

Laws of Leadership Series, Volume III

The 7 Golden Rules of
MILTON HERSHEY

Published by
Executive Books
206 West Allen Street
Mechanicsburg, PA 17055
717-766-9499   800-233-2665
Fax: 717-766-6565
www.ExecutiveBooks.com

Copyright © 2005 Executive Books
All rights reserved.

ISBN-13: 978-1-933715-45-2
ISBN-10: 1-933715-45-6

Cover Design and Interior Layout
by Gregory Dixon

Printed in the United States of America

Table of Contents

Foreword

MILTON S. HERSHEY
"His deeds are his monument.
His life is our inspiration."

These words are emblazoned at the base of the statue of Milton S. Hershey erected by the Alumni of the Milton Hershey School. The school was established by Milton and Catherine in 1909 and today serves nearly 1,500 boys and girls whose parents are unable to provide care for the child.

The words neatly summarize Hershey's life. A poor, inadequately educated boy, he combined a life of amazing entrepreneurship with a desire to leave all his wealth for the benefit of others. The world knows his name as it refers to a wonderful legacy—chocolate. Over 8,000 grateful graduates of the school bless his name for the opportunity it bestowed. Millions know his town, his entertainment complex and its hospitality industry.

All this was made possible because one person believed in the power of a reasonably priced product, mass produced and distributed just as did his fellow industrialists Henry Ford, Thomas Edison, George Eastman, Alexander Graham Bell and W.W. Kellogg.

Truly the vision of one man exemplified the face of entrepreneurship and philanthropy. That man was Milton S. Hershey.

Richard Zimmerman
Former Chairman and CEO
Hershey Foods

Introduction

The terms "industrial magnate" and "factory town" conjure up turn-of-the century names like Mellon, Carnegie and Rockefeller, and images of opulent living contrasted to the miserable economic conditions of the era. Yet one man of that time who fit the broader stereotype behaved differently than most of his wealthy contemporaries.

Milton Snavely Hershey, commonly referred to as "The Chocolate King," was born in 1857 in Dauphin County, Pennsylvania, and raised among the "Plain People" of the Mennonite faith. Hershey was to chocolate what Henry Ford was to the automobile, and he can rightfully be called the founder of the American chocolate industry. Today, the Hershey empire in southeastern Pennsylvania includes a school, university medical center, amusement park, museum, zoo, semiprofessional hockey team, hotel, two world-class golf courses and the world's largest manufacturer of chocolate. The town of Hershey itself is a legacy to a very successful man who provided for his workers. It stemmed from his desire to create a kind of paradise that met all his factory workers' needs.

Hershey's passion for chocolate was matched by his love for children. Having come from a broken household and unable to have children with his wife, he founded a school for disadvantaged youth that aimed to provide a solid education in a warm, reassuring atmosphere.

Greg Rothman

When M.S. was still a toddler there was a large sign standing in a barren field a stone's throw from the Cocoa House. On it in big letters were these words, "HERSHEY MEANS PROGRESS." The words would be prophetic.

When I left home as a boy to tackle the job of making a living my mother gave me some good advice. She said, "Milton, you are now going out into the world to make a man of yourself. My best advice to you is – when you tackle a job stick to it until you have mastered it." I never have forgotten those words and now when I think of the chocolate business and the way it has grown I think it was my mother's advice that spurred me on and helped me to overcome my obstacles.

When I failed in New York City I was able to pay my creditors forty cents on the dollar. As soon as I got on my feet financially I returned to New York City and paid my creditors the remaining sixty percent of my indebtedness. I never did anything since that gave me as much satisfaction as when I paid back that money.

He bought the most expensive, most impressive and most modern machinery he could find, but had no one to show him how to use this equipment. After moving to Derry Township to conduct his research in private, he worked behind closed doors with a guard watching while he experimented with various formulas.

"Why shouldn't I work!" he replied when he was asked why he did not sit back and take things easier. "I'm still on the payroll and I don't want to lose my job, especially at this late date."

Hershey often ventured out to the job site (he was always at work before anyone else). On one occasion, the foreman approached Hershey and proudly reported that a newly acquired machine was doing the work of 40 men. "Then get rid of it and get those men back," Hershey commanded.

You can only make money by giving people what they want, and by making good use of your opportunities. When I started making chocolate I didn't follow the policies of those already in the business. If I had, I would never have made a go of it. Instead, I started out with the determination to make a better nickel chocolate bar than any of my competitors made, and I did so.

Hershey's only advertising was the product itself: "Give them quality," he would say. "That's the best advertising in the world."

Hershey invested all the profits from the sale to expand his chocolate making, saying, "I'll stake everything on chocolate." He confided in friends, "Caramels are just a fad. The chocolate market will be a permanent one."

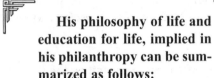

His philosophy of life and education for life, implied in his philanthropy can be summarized as follows:

1. Young man, be honest! Here is the pivotal point in one's relationship to others.

2. Young man, train yourself for useful work! Here is the basis for one's relationship to his economic environment.

3. Young man, love God and your fellowman! Here is the cardinal principle of life."

Unbroken String of Failures That Led to Success

Hershey began life as the only son of an unlikely and ultimately incompatible couple, Henry Hershey and Fanny Snavely. Henry was an unreliable but innovative father who loved books and spent his life wandering, enthralled with the new. His life was filled with ideas, many of which came to pass, though not by his hand. Henry Hershey's life was marked by failure and a lack of perseverance, but not for a lack of trying. Henry gave his son eternal optimism, even in the face of constant failure. This trait would serve Milton well through the early years of his candy-making ventures.

Fanny, on the other hand, was a forceful, hardworking, some would say humorless woman who one day was left with no one but Milton to whom to dedicate her life. Henry left her when Milton was young; their daughter, Serena, died at the age of four. Fanny believed, like her fellow Mennonites, that working hard represented devotion to God and that wealth was a sign of God's grace. To his benefit and perhaps unwittingly, Milton united these disparate strains and became both innovative and hardworking.

During Milton's childhood his family was almost always broke and constantly on the move. His father, Henry, wanted Milton educated, while his mother Fanny feared the modern. Fanny's father was a Mennonite religious leader. Milton attended seven different schools during an eight year period: from

Milton S. Hershey Golden Rule #1:
Think Outside The Box

When I started making chocolate I didn't follow the policies of those already in the business. If I had, I would never have made a go of it. Instead, I started out with the determination to make a better nickel chocolate bar than any of my competitors made, and I did so.

Milton Hershey

The firefly only shines when on the wing; so it is with the mind; when we rest we darken.
Aristotle

I can give you a six-word formula for success: Think things through—then follow through.
Capt. Edward V. Rickenbacker

Great men are they who see that spiritual is stronger than any material force—that thoughts rule the world.
Ralph Waldo Emerson

Mind is the great lever of all things; human thought is the process by which human ends are alternately answered.
Daniel Webster

free-thinking to puritan. He received the equivalent of a fourth grade education.

For a time, the Hersheys traveled where Henry's wanderings took them, which meant that Milton's education was sporadic. He did not do well in school, nor did he enjoy it. After the fourth grade, with encouragement from his book-suspicious mother, Milton left school. Milton and his mother depended on the generosity of family members. Later Milton would borrow money from his uncles and aunts.

His distaste for reading and writing left him essentially illiterate and left the world without a personal written record of his life or beliefs. However, his life, full of deeds, serves as a text for what was important to Hershey. Ronald D. Glosser, former president and chief executive officer for the Hershey Trust Company, calls Milton Hershey "a common man with an uncommon touch."

When M.S. was still a toddler there was a large sign standing in a barren field a stone's throw from the Cocoa House. On it in big letters were these words, "HERSHEY MEANS PROGRESS." The words would be prophetic. From a string of failures to success in Lancaster to Derry Township, Europe, Cuba, building factories in Pennsylvania, running railroads and sugar mills in Cuba, laying out towns and golf courses, running stores, hotels, utilities, and founding schools for orphans in Pennsylvania and Cuba: Hershey meant progress.

As a small boy, Milton would go with his parents into the City of Harrisburg to the market. While his parents sold their farm goods at a stand, M.S. would sneak

Milton S. Hershey Golden Rule #1:
Think Outside The Box

What you think means more than anything else in your life. More than what you earn, more than where you live, more than your social position, and more than what anyone else may think about you.
George Matthew Adams

Creative thinking is today's most prized, profit-producing possession for any individual, corporation or country. It has the capacity to change you, your business and the world.
Robert P. Crawford

For I say, through the grace given unto me, to every man that is among you, not to think of himself more highly than he ought to think; but to think soberly, according as God hath dealt to every man the measure of faith.
Romans 12:3

Thinking is creating with God., as thinking is writing with the ready writer, and worlds are only leaves turned over in the process of composition, about his throne.
H.W. Beecher

around the corner to a little confectionery store to buy "sour balls." His lifelong love of candy and sweets had begun. Some people have a "sweet-tooth." Milton S. Hershey had a whole mouth full of sweet teeth.

"When I left home as a boy to tackle the job of making a living my mother gave me some good advice. She said, 'Milton, you are now going out into the world to make a man of yourself. My best advice to you is – when you tackle a job stick to it until you have mastered it.' I never have forgotten those words and now when I think of the chocolate business and the way it has grown I think it was my mother's advice that spurred me on and helped me to overcome my obstacles."

After a four-year apprenticeship to Lancaster confectioner Joseph Royer, Milton was encouraged to go out on his own. His Aunt Mattie provided $150 in venture capital. On June 1, 1876, as America prepared for its centennial celebration, the 18-year-old Hershey opened his first candy business, choosing Philadelphia over Lancaster. He set up shop in a little brick house at 935 Spring Garden Street. M.S., as he was called, worked all night making candy that he sold by day, with his mother and aunt often laboring by his side. Despite his hard work and the success of the penny candy, called French Secrets (a message was wrapped with the candy), it was not enough to pay his expenses. Sugar dealers were unwilling to give him credit and the

Milton S. Hershey Golden Rule #2:
Perseverance

"When I left home as a boy to tackle the job of making a living my mother gave me some good advice. She said, 'Milton, you are now going out into the world to make a man of yourself. My best advice to you is – when you tackle a job stick to it until you have mastered it.' I never have forgotten those words and now when I think of the chocolate business and the way it has grown I think it was my mother's advice that spurred me on and helped me to overcome my obstacles." **—Milton S. Hershey**

Diligence, as it avails in all things, is also of the utmost moment in pleading causes. Diligence is to be particularly cultivated by us; it is to be constantly exerted, it is capable of effecting almost everything.
Cicero

A determination to succeed is the only way to succeed that I know anything about.
William Feather

Keep on going, and the chances are that you will stumble on something, perhaps when you are at least expecting it. I never heard of anyone ever stumbling on something sitting down.
Charles F. Kettering

price of cane was high. (This experience forged in Hershey a lifelong concern about the cost of sugar cane.) After seven struggling years, and in debt to his relatives, he closed his shop.

Hershey moved to Denver, where his father was working in the silver mines. He found a job with another candy maker, where he learned the priceless secret of mixing fresh milk into caramels, which extended the shelf life and enhanced the flavor of the candy. One can only imagine that the milk made M.S. think of the unlimited and high quality liquid produced by the diary cows in Central Pennsylvania. From Denver, Hershey moved briefly to Chicago with his father, where he found too much competition in the industry.

He also tried New Orleans, but discovered that it would be too expensive to move his candy-making machines from Philadelphia. Concluding that it would be cheaper to open a shop in New York City, Hershey moved there and began working at Huyler's, a well-known confectioner. Every evening he made batches of taffy in his landlady's kitchen. He put the wrapped taffy pieces in a basket and sold them on the streets. His mother and Aunt Mattie again arrived to help with the business.

Hershey decided to take a risk and acquire cough drop machinery on credit. Though he learned the manufacturing steps that he would later use to mass-produce chocolate (which up until then had been a handmade luxury item), the cough drop business failed; he had only enough money to send his mother and aunt home.

"When I failed in New York City I was able
to pay my creditors forty cents on the dollar. As

Milton S. Hershey Golden Rule #2:
Perseverance

Persistence is what makes the impossible possible, the possible likely, and the likely definite.
Robert Half

Perseverance is more prevailing than violence; and many things which cannot be overcome when they are together, yield themselves up when taken little by little.
Plutarch

By perseverance the snail reached the Ark.
Charles H. Spurgeon

An ounce of application is worth a ton of abstraction.
Booker T. Washington

Overcome a hard job, overcome a difficult and discouraging job; fight, fight, fight, never stop!
John Wanamaker

Hard pounding, gentleman; but we will see who can pound the longest.
Arthur Wellesley, Duke of Wellington

soon as I got on my feet financially I returned to New York City and paid my creditors the remaining sixty percent of my indebtedness. I never did anything since that gave me as much satisfaction as when I paid back that money."

When he later returned to Lancaster, his uncles (and former patrons) refused to give him any more money or a place to stay. His friend and former employee, William "Lebbie" Lebkicher, took him in and paid for the shipping of his machinery. Lebkicher was a Civil War veteran who believed in Milton's dreams. (Years later, at Lebkicher's funeral, Hershey said, "We just buried the best friend I ever had.")

With five failures behind him and out of money (a self-described "unbroken string of failures"), Hershey could easily have given up. But his lifelong affinity for sweets, coupled with his persevering nature, caused him to press on.

Hershey worked for sixteen hours a day, starting at 4:30 am milking cows. He worked long hours his entire life. In the beginning he would make his candy at night and sell it during the day.

He tried again in his native countryside of Lancaster. Here, he finally had his first success, "Crystal A Caramels," in 1886. His luck had turned when a mysterious British importer placed a large order and Hershey persuaded a skeptical local bank to loan him the money to fill it. By the 1890s, Hershey's caramel company had made him a millionaire. His factory covered a Lancaster city block. Hershey's only advertising was the product itself: "Give them quality,"

Milton S. Hershey Golden Rule #3:
Hard Work

"Why shouldn't I work!" he replied when he was asked why he did not sit back and take things easier. "I'm still on the payroll and I don't want to lose my job, especially at this late date."

Milton S. Hershey

No fine work can be done without concentration and self-sacrifice and toil and doubt.
Max Beerbohm

Whatsoever thy hand findeth to do, do it with thy might; for there is no work, nor device, nor knowledge, nor wisdom, in the grave, whither thou goest.
Ecclesiastes 9:10

Nobody can think straight who does not work. Idleness warps the mind. Thinking without constructive action becomes a disease.
Henry Ford

I early found that when I worked for myself alone, myself alone worked for me; but when I worked for others also, others worked also for me.
Benjamin Franklin

he would say. "That's the best advertising in the world."

In 1899, a group of competing caramel manufacturers approached Hershey about creating a broad alliance to take control of the industry. While he had no interest in merging, Hershey had become increasingly interested in chocolate and offered to sell his company, which he did the following year for a million dollars, sagaciously retaining the rights to make his chocolate.

Hershey invested all the profits from the sale to expand his chocolate making, saying, "I'll stake everything on chocolate." He confided in friends, "Caramels are just a fad. The chocolate market will be a permanent one."

> "Originally I planned to build my factory in Lancaster, but the property owners wanted too much money for their sites, so I looked elsewhere. I inspected locations in four states, and it was not until then that I was convinced that Derry Township was the most suitable place for me to build the factory.
>
> "When my friends learned that I was going to build the factory up here they thought I had gone out of my mind."

Hershey had succeeded with caramels by adding fresh whole milk to improve the quality of the candy. He believed he could outdo his European counterparts—so he ignored the old masters who had been laboring over the delicate and expensive production of chocolate for centuries. He had no background in chemistry to develop a formula for making his chocolate, everything was simply

Milton S. Hershey Golden Rule #3:
Hard Work

But let every man prove his own work, and then shall he have rejoicing in himself alone, and not in another.
Galatians 6:4

We work to become, not to acquire.
Elbert Hubbard

If you want to leave your footprints on the sands of time, be sure you're wearing work shoes.
Italian Proverb

If you intend to go to work, there is no better place than right where you are; if you do not intend to go to work, you cannot get along anywhere. Squirming and crawling about from place to place can do no good.
Abraham Lincoln

The highest reward for a person's toil is not what he gets for it, but what he becomes by it.
John Ruskin

I never work hard when I am working; I only work hard when I am not working.
Irving Caesar

trial and error. He bought the most expensive, most impressive and most modern machinery he could find, but had no one to show him how to use this equipment. After moving to Derry Township to conduct his research in private, he worked behind closed doors with a guard watching while he experimented with various formulas.

Milton Hershey had tasted many European milk chocolates (all too expensive to be purchased by the masses), and with the help of equipment he obtained from a supplier in Dresden, Germany—he visited milk chocolate manufacturers in Britain, Germany, Switzerland, and France. However, when Hershey decided to manufacture his own milk chocolate, he consciously decided not to follow the methods the Europeans had perfected.

While Hershey was on the verge of success in revolutionizing the chocolate industry, his personal life was less sweet. Often lonely, with few friends, the 41-year-old Hershey seemed destined to remain the eternal bachelor.

Hershey reportedly looked in the mirror one day and said: "M.S., you're a fool, a diamond covered fop in a loud suit." But shortly after, his luck changed when he met and fell in love with the beautiful Catherine Elizabeth "Kitty" Sweeney of Jamestown, New York. Sweeney, a 25-year-old from an Irish Catholic family of modest means, was cheerful and witty, with a disarming smile and bright blue eyes. The two were married in the rectory at Saint Patrick's Cathedral in New York City in May 1898.

Milton S. Hershey Golden Rule #4:
Take Risks

He bought the most expensive, most impressive and most modern machinery he could find, but had no one to show him how to use this equipment. After moving to Derry Township to conduct his research in private, he worked behind closed doors with a guard watching while he experimented with various formulas.

Hershey decided to take a risk and acquire cough drop machinery on credit.

It is better by a noble boldness to run the risk of being subject to half of the evils we anticipate, than to remain in cowardly listlessness for fear of what may happen.
Herodotus

Every man is bold when his whole fortune is at stake.
Dionysus of Halicarnassus

Whatever you do, or dream you can do, begin it. Boldness has genius, power and magic in it.
Johann Wolfgang von Goethe

Put a grain of boldness in everything you do.
Baltasar Gracián

Unlike her husband, Kitty was full of *joie de vivre*. Hershey was raised by a woman whose view of the world did not easily include this refreshing quality of indulgence. Indeed, he may never have encountered such spirit until meeting Kitty. Predictably, she received a cool reception from Fanny, who asked upon meeting her, "Were you ever on the stage?"

In 1903, the couple returned to Hershey's birthplace of Derry Township, 13 miles east of Harrisburg, where Hershey, his business prospering, set out to build the ideal town for his factory workers. He included every amenity, creating what could be called a "New Jerusalem," with perfectly executed streets, parks, homes, rail service, trolley lines—even an amusement park. This unprecedented endeavor found his contemporaries, even associates, unfavorably dumbstruck at Hershey's gargantuan vision and "wasted" money. But Hershey's life was ruled by the long-instilled Biblical maxim of doing unto others as you would have them do unto you. He believed that there was a greater good than personal success and comfort.

Success was a new dance for Hershey. When he found it, he was relentless in retaining it. Democratizing chocolate was not enough; he continued to perfect production, creating new machines, from mixing to wrapping. With each new triumph, workers would hear his voice ring out, "We've got it!" (They would also hear Hershey say, "Boys, don't rock the boat, row it.") Hershey was also fond of saying, "You can't keep the corners brushed up if you don't keep after them with a broom."

Milton S. Hershey Golden Rule #4:
Take Risks

Only the bold get to the top.
Publilius Syrus

Boldness becomes rarer, the higher the rank.
Karl von Clausewitz

There are some things one can only achieve by a deliberate leap in the opposite direction.
Franz Kafka

Both fortune and love befriend the bold.
Ovid

Courage consists, not in blindly overlooking danger, but in seeing and conquering it.
Jean Paul Friedrich Richter

When a decision has to be made, make it. There is no totally right time for anything.
General George Patton

Make your decision, make it yours, and live and die by it.
Charlie "Tremendous" Jones

Hershey did not regard his wealth as a just reward for hard work, singular virtue, consummate genius or the other surpassing merits which are usually catalogued. To Mr. Hershey wealth "just came."

Industrial success alone was not enough for Kitty, either. After sadly realizing that they would never have children, Kitty urged M.S. to create a school for disadvantaged children. In what they considered the capstone of their lives, the Hersheys founded The Industrial School on November 15, 1909; it admitted its first pupils, four orphan boys, the following year, using Hershey's birthplace, The Homestead, as both home and school. The original idea for the orphanage came from Kitty. They deeded 485 acres of farmland, including the Homestead. After Kitty died too young at 42, M.S. donated his entire estate to the Hershey Trust for the benefit of the school. At the time the gift was worth over $60 million and kept secret from the public.

With his unstable, nomadic childhood and separated parents, Hershey empathized with orphans. His goal for the school was to provide for children an opportunity for a quality education, a wholesome environment and a loving, caring atmosphere. Still thriving today, the Milton Hershey School has 1,100 students enrolled from throughout the United States. The central campus encompasses more than 3,000 acres, including farmland, streams, ponds and woodlands. Ninety-seven student homes are located throughout the campus, staffed by house-parents whose job is to create stability, express love, and instill discipline, moral values and a work ethic in a family atmosphere.

Milton S. Hershey Golden Rule #5:
Take Care of Your Workers

Hershey often ventured out to the job site (he was always at work before anyone else). On one occasion, the foreman approached Hershey and proudly reported that a newly acquired machine was doing the work of 40 men. "Then get rid of it and get those men back," Hershey commanded.

You can employ men and hire hands to work for you, but you will have to win their hearts to have them work with you.
WIlliam J.H. Boetcker

It marks a big step in a man's development when he comes to realize that other men can be called in to help him do a better job than he can do alone.
Andrew Carnegie

The man who builds a factory builds a temple; the man who works there worships there; and to each is due not scorn and blame but reverence and praise.
Calvin Coolidge

We would rather have one man or woman working with us than three merely working for us.
J. Dabney Day

The Hershey School Trust, created to preserve Kitty and Milton's vision, administers their fortune according to their guidelines. Hershey once said his life would be complete if just 50 young people benefited from his school. Today, the school boasts 7,100 alumni. One former student and employee remarks, "If Hershey were here today, I would get down on my knees and thank him for the good he did in my life."

In 1918, Hershey put his $60 million fortune in trust for the school. The bequest was held in confidence until 1923, when it was discovered and revealed by *The New York Times*. Despite his efforts at altruistic anonymity, Hershey was also known locally for his generosity. Hershey community archivist Pamela Cassidy notes that "many who knew Hershey said his essence was evident in his town and school." He would often sit down with the Derry Township School District at year's end and write a check to balance its books. The enormity of his donations contrasts to the $54,000 price tag of his mansion, "Highpoint," which he had built for himself and Kitty. Ultimately, after Kitty's death, he even donated Highpoint to the Hershey Country Club to be used as its clubhouse. While golfers roamed the dining rooms below, Hershey used three small rooms upstairs. After he died, his personal effects were auctioned for a mere $20,000.

Some time after the school was created, Kitty took ill with a rare neurological disease. She grew increasingly weaker as she fought the illness with traditional and non-traditional remedies. During her illness, Milton brought roses for her every day. When she died in 1915 at the age

Milton S. Hershey Golden Rule #5:
Take Care of Your Workers

Many times a day I realize how my own outer and inner life is built upon the labors of my fellow men, both living and dead, and how earnestly I must exert myself to return as much as I have received.
Albert Einstein

Next to us is not the workman whom we have hired, with whom we love so well to talk, but the workman whose work we are.
Henry David Thoreau

Mighty of heart, mighty of mind, magnanimous— to be this is indeed to be great in life.
John Ruskin

It is the duty of a man of honor to teach others the good which he has not been able to do himself because of the malignity of the times, that this good finally can be done by another more loved in heaven.
Niccolò Machiavelli

I expect to pass through this life but once. If therefore, there be any kindness I can show, or any good thing I can do to any fellow being, let me do it now, and not defer or neglect it, as I shall not pass this way again.
William Penn

of 42, her nurse reported that Hershey was "like a madman." For 17 years, he had tasted that sweetness for which he had longed. Once again, at 58, Hershey became the austere, duty-driven man of his earlier years. He never remarried.

His attentions now turned toward Cuba. Hershey traveled there in 1916 with his mother, who eventually maintained an apartment in Havana. He was enchanted by the country. He strolled through the streets, viewing the old fortifications of Havana Harbor, the city wall, the Spanish Cathedral. Here, he also discovered an avenue for uninterrupted, autonomous sugar production, acquiring numerous sugar cane plantations and mills. By the time Hershey died, his company's Cuban operations exceeded 65,000 acres.

At first, the Cubans watched Hershey's business acquisitions with suspicion. He had sugar districts in Central San Juan Bautista, Central Rosario, Central Carmen, Central San Antonio and Central Jesus Maria. Hershey opened the Hershey Cuban Railroad and bought a 100-year-old Spanish hacienda at Rosario for his personal use. The house was beautifully tiled and furnished and had a 10-acre garden. Hershey started a school, the Cuban Orphan School, at Central Rosario, which served the same purpose as his school in Pennsylvania. He also provided well for his Cuban workers, as he had for his other employees.

In 1933, at the Presidential Palace in Havana, Cuban president Gerardo Machado awarded Hershey the country's highest honor for a non-national, the Grand Cross of

Milton S. Hershey Golden Rule #6:
Give to Live

Hershey's life was ruled by the long-instilled Biblical maxim of doing unto others as you would have them do unto you. He believed that there was a greater good than personal success and comfort.

A man there was, and they called him mad; the more he gave, the more he had.
John Bunyan

We make a living by what we get, we make a life by what we give.
Winston Churchill

No person has ever been honored for what he received. Honor has been the reward for what he gave.
Calvin Coolidge

No man who continues to add something to the material, intellectual and moral well-being of the place in which he lives is left long without proper reward.
Booker T. Washington

the National Order of Carlos Manuel de Céspedes. In presenting it, Machado said, "With this medal we give a bit of our soul; with it goes our lasting admiration."

The Hotel Hershey was built during the Great Depression. Overlooking the town, it is magnificent with its marble corridors, royal suites, grandiose fountains and botanical gardens. The gardens overflow with roses, including one created in Kitty's name. As the rest of the country struggled to find jobs, Hershey insisted on putting people to work, breaking ground for the substantial structures of "Chocolatetown, U.S.A." during the depths of the Depression. In addition to the hotel, Hershey ordered built a community center, a senior hall (the present Milton Hershey High School), his administration offices, the Hershey Arena and the Parkview Golf Course Club House, all constructed between 1929 and 1933. Hershey employees never missed a payday. During the construction of the hotel, Hershey often ventured out to the job site (he was always at work before anyone else). On one occasion, the foreman approached Hershey and proudly reported that a newly acquired machine was doing the work of 40 men. "Then get rid of it and get those men back," Hershey commanded.

Hershey continued to work as hard as ever. He would often announce, "If I rest, I'll rust."

"Why shouldn't I work!" he replied when he was asked why he did not sit back and take things easier. "I'm still on the payroll and I don't want to lose my job, especially at this late date." Strange as it may seem, Mr. Hershey was never on the payroll, his income came from the shares of stock he owned personally.

Milton S. Hershey Golden Rule #6:
Give to Live

Give, and it shall be given unto you; good measure, pressed down, and shaken together, and running over, shall men give unto your bosom. For with the same measure that ye mete withal it shall be measured to you again.
Luke 6:38

If there be any truer measure of a man than by what he does, it must be by what he gives.
Robert South

We are rich only through what we give: and poor only through what we refuse and keep.
Anne Swetchine

Generosity during life is a very different thing from generosity in the hour of death; one proceeds from genuine liberality, and benevolence; the other from pride or fear, or from the fact that you cannot take your money with you to the other world.
Horace Mann

Hershey continued producing chocolate during the Depression with the intention of maintaining an affordable product that would brighten a discouraged country's day. With the onset of the Second World War, Hershey's staff created non-melting chocolate bars for the military, called Field Ration "D." The "D" represented "daily," and as the United States entered the war, the Hershey Chocolate Factory was making half a million chocolate bars per day.

Arman F. Leo, a highly decorated veteran and native of Dauphin County, has fond memories of the Ration "D" bar: "Sitting alone in a foxhole was the best time to eat the 'D' bar. They seemed to last all night. We gave them out to the children in Africa, Italy and France. We were greeted like Santa Claus."

The Hershey name and GI goodwill was spread throughout the world by the Ration "D" bar. The international love for Hershey's chocolate was bolstered by the military's unintentional marketing of the Hershey bar. Mr. Hershey was particularly pleased when the company was given the Army Navy "E" Production Award from the U.S. Government, the first of only five such awards. Nearly a month and a half after Japan's surrender ended the war, the 88-year-old Hershey died of heart failure on Oct. 13, 1945.

His good friend, Richard Murrie said, "He was a philanthropist in the true sense of the word. He got far more satisfaction out of giving the money to the school than out of spending it himself."

He followed the advice he gave to others. "Whatever money you boys earn during your lifetime, use it wisely.

Milton S. Hershey Golden Rule #7:
Your Life is Your Legacy

Twenty-five years before he died, Milton Hershey gave everything away. He did not just give to get for the sake of getting. He gave so that he could be capable of giving more.

After he died, Milton S. Hershey's personal effects were auctioned for a mere $20,000.

The great business of life is to be, to do without and to depart.
John Morley

He who wishes to fulfill his mission in the world must be a man of one idea, that is of one great overmastering purpose, overshadowing all his aims, and guiding and controlling his entire life.
Julius Bates

A man's biography is written in terms not so much of what he causes to happen, but rather what happens to him and in him. The difference between men is not in the adversity which comes to them, but rather how they meet the adversity.
Fulton Sheen

Spend it for the good of others, and you will be richly rewarded." Hard work, generosity and honesty were the three principles of Milton Hershey's life and success. Mr. Murrie said, "the greatest single factor of Mr. Hershey's success has been the inflexible policy of honesty inculcated into the business."

Hershey saw his success differently. "Some people think that I've had an easy time of it. They say that I have the Hershey luck, whatever that is, and as a result money flowed into my lap. But luck had nothing to do with my success."

He added, "As I see it, my success is the result of not being satisfied with mediocrity, and in making the most of my opportunities."

Others who were close to him saw the obvious and not so obvious. W. Allen Hammond, the Principal at the Milton Hershey School from 1934 to 1959 knew M.S. well and wrote about what made him great:

> "The profits came only after hard work and perseverance. Mr. Hershey was a tireless worker. He worked hard and long, unwilling to accept defeat or to let good enough alone. The greater the difficulty, the greater the challenge to his indefatigable energy. When he fell in failure, he seemed always to have fallen forward. He may have been down for a while, but the rebound invariably placed him on a higher level from which to start all over again.
>
> "Mr. Hershey, it seems to me, kept on center in his relationships toward God, his fellowman,

Milton S. Hershey Golden Rule #7:
Your Life is Your Legacy

In some measure all that comes after you is going to be influenced and determined by the kind of life you make in your business of living. When reviewed from such a height of vision, even the seemingly least important life gathers round it a glory which truly passes understanding.

Laurence I. Neale, D.D.

The greatest thing in the world is a human life; the greatest work in the world is the helpful touch upon that life. The look, the word, the invisible atmosphere of the home and the church, the sights and sounds of all the busy days enter the supersensitive and retentive soul, and are woven into the life tissue.

Charles Lamoureux

The gratification of wealth is not found in mere possession or in lavish expenditure, but in wise application.

Miguel de Cervantes

and the world. His philosophy of life and education for life, implied in his philanthropy can be summarized as follows:

1. Young man, be honest! Here is the pivotal point in one's relationship to others.

2. Young man, train yourself for useful work! Here is the basis for one's relationship to his economic environment.

3. Young man, love God and your fellow-man! Here is the cardinal principle of life."

Today, visitors to the town of Hershey are greeted by the tantalizing smell of fresh milk chocolate being produced in the heart of town. Chocolate Avenue remains a quiet yet active commercial main artery, with eclectic architectural tributes to the man who built it. Since 1963, the street has been lined with lights topped with large Hershey Kiss replicas. Each year, thousands of eager tourists make their way through the model factory, "Chocolate World," in mechanized boats that take them through a pictorial journey of the chocolate manufacturing process. Throughout the town, the motto of the Milton Hershey School is repeated: "His deeds are his monument. His life is our inspiration."

Norman Vincent Peale, visiting the town in 1989 to give a speech, was touring the Founder's Hall (the Hershey school auditorium built in 1970) when a teacher asked him if he would take a minute to address

Milton S. Hershey Golden Rule #7:
Your Life is Your Legacy

A well-ordered life is like climbing a tower; the view halfway up is better than the view from the base, and it steadily becomes finer as the horizon expands.
William Lyon Phelps

The whole earth is the tomb of heroic men, and their story is not graven only on stone over their clay, but abides everywhere, without a visible symbol, woven into the stuff of other men's lives.
Thucydides

Our whole life should speak forth our thankfulness; every condition and place we are in should be a witness of our thankfulness. This will make the times and places we live in better for us. When we ourselves are monuments of God's mercy, it is fit we should be patterns of His praises, and leave monuments to others. We should think it given to us to do something better than to live in. We live not to live: our life is not the end of itself, but the praise of the giver.
R. Libbes

his students. With the life-sized bronze statue of Hershey with one of his schoolboys as the backdrop, Peale asked, "How many of you would like to have millions of dollars someday?" The children all raised their hands high in the air. "And, how many of you would, 25 years before you die, give it all away to strangers?" After seeing that not a single hand was raised, Peale looked over his shoulder and said, "Hershey did just that."

When one delves into Mr. Hershey's life, with its ups and downs, and studies his untiring efforts at work, his quaint views of life, his ever-ready willingness to help his fellowmen and workers, his modesty over his business successes, and the beautiful town he has built, one cannot help but realize that he was a man of the most unusual type.

> "You can only make money by giving people what they want, and by making good use of your opportunities. When I started making chocolate I didn't follow the policies of those already in the business. If I had, I would never have made a go of it. Instead, I started out with the determination to make a better nickel chocolate bar than any of my competitors made, and I did so."

On Sept. 13, 1995, the 138th anniversary of Hershey's birth (and 50 years after his death), the U.S. Postal Service honored him with a stamp. More than 5,000 children, alumni, Hershey employees and admirers joined Postmaster General Marvin Runyon in officially

Milton S. Hershey Golden Rule #7:
Your Life is Your Legacy

A good man doubles the length of his existence; to have lived so as to have looked back with pleasure on our past life is to live twice.
Martial

Live your life each day as you would climb a mountain. An occasional glance toward the summit keeps the goal in mind, but many beautiful scenes are to be observed from each new vantage point. Climb slowly, steadily, enjoying each passing moment; and the view from the summit will serve as a fitting climax for the journey.
Harold V. Melchert

Biographies of great, but especially of good men, are most instructive and useful as helps, guides, and incentives to others. Some of the best are almost equivalent to gospels—teaching high living, high thinking, and energetic actions for their own and the world's good.
Samuel Smiles

dedicating the stamp at a ceremony at the Hersheypark Arena. Runyon said of the honoree, "He possessed the one thing sweeter and more pure than even his chocolate—a loving heart."

He hath sent me to bind up the broken hearted as one whom his mother comforteth, so will I comfort you . . .

Yea, they may forget, yet will I not forget thee.

The Prophet Isaiah

LIFE-CHANGING CLASSICS

As A Man Thinketh	James Allen
The Reason Why	R. A. Laidlaw
A Message To Garcia	Elbert Hubbard
That Something	William Woodbridge
Acres Of Diamonds	Russell Conwell
Bradford, You're Fired!	William Woodbridge
Maxims of Life and Business	John Wanamaker
Books Are Tremendous	Charlie "T" Jones
Advantages of Poverty	Andrew Carnegie
Succeeding With What You Have	Charles Schwab

LAWS OF LEADERSHIP

Character Building	Booker T. Washington
Self-Improvement Through Public Speaking	Orison Marden

COMING SOON

The Thirteen Success Principles	Ben Franklin
The Price of Leadership	Charlie "T" Jones
Sizzle Your Way Through Life The Wheeler Way	Dr. Ben Kai
The Greatest Thing in the World	Henry Drummond

PERSONAL DEVELOPMENT CLASSICS

You and Your Network	Smith
The Power of Positive Thinking	Peale
How to Win Friends and Influence People	Carnegie
Think and Grow Rich	Hill
I Dare You	Danforth
The Go-Getter	Kyne
How I Raised Myself From Failure to Success	Bettger
The Greatest Salesman in the World	Mandino
Move Ahead With Possibility Thinking	Schuler
Life is Tremendous	Jones
See You at the Top	Ziglar
The Success System That Never Fails	Stone
The Secret of Success	Allen
The Richest Man in Babylon	Clason
The Ultimate Gift	Stovall
Freedom From Fear	Matteson
How to Win Over Worry	Haggai
Napoleon Hill's Magic Ladder to Success	Hill
Believe and Achieve	Stone
One Minute Millionaire	Hansen
Ten Things I Learned From Bill Porter	Brady
There Are No Limits	Cox
Now Is Your Time To Win	Dean
Positive Impact	Reid
Millionaire Mentor	Reid
Leadership Lessons Learned by the Impossible Dreamer	Mitchell-Halter
It Takes Less Than One Minute to Suit Up For The Lord	Blanchard